The POSITIVE POWER of the 10 COMMANDMENTS

PHYLLIS STILLWELL PROKOP

BROADMAN PRESS
Nashville, Tennessee

1987

© Copyright 1987 • Broadman Press
All rights reserved

4250-37
ISBN: 0-8054-5037-8

Dewey Decimal Classification: 222.16
Subject Heading: TEN COMMANDMENTS
Library of Congress Catalog Card Number: 86-31043
Printed in the United States of America

Unless otherwise indicated Scripture quotations are from the Revised Standard Version of the Bible, copyrighted 1946, 1952, © 1971, 1973. Quotations marked (KJV) are from the King James Version of the Bible.

Library of Congress Cataloging-in-Publication Data

Prokop, Phyllis Stillwell.
    The positive power of the 10 commandments.

    1. Ten commandments.   I. Title.   II. Title: Positive
power of the Ten commandments.
BV4655.P73   1987   241.5′2   86-31043
ISBN 0-8054-5037-8

Dedication

For our two beloved sons
who bring us much joy:

Dr. Charles Kent Prokop
and
Bert Kimball Prokop

Preface

The Ten Commandments are God's guidelines for the good and fulfilling life. They are not, as many think, negative robbers designed to remove all joy and pleasure. They may, in fact, be viewed as road signs placed by a totally loving hand to direct the traveler with reminders to Drive here! Walk here! Travel here, for this is the road of relaxation and peace.

The purpose of this book is to look beyond the commands to that beautiful field of blessing waiting for the trusting and obedient traveler who views the instructions positively and weaves them into a texture of an enriched and achieving life

PHYLLIS STILLWELL PROKOP

Contents

Exodus 20:1-17

1 And God spoke all these words, saying,

2 "I am the Lord your God, who brought you out of the land of Egypt, out of the house of bondage.

3 "You shall have no other gods before me.

4 "You shall not make for yourself a graven image, or any likeness of anything that is in the earth beneath, or that is in the water under the earth; ⁵you shall not bow down to them or serve them; for I the Lord your God am a jealous God, visiting the iniquity of the fathers upon the children to the third and the fourth generation of those who hate me, ⁶but showing steadfast love to thousands of those who love me and keep my commandments.

7 "You shall not take the name of the Lord your God in vain; for the Lord will not hold him guiltless who takes his name in vain.

8 "Remember the sabbath day, to keep it holy. ⁹Six days you shall labor, and do all your work; ¹⁰but the seventh day is a sabbath to the Lord your God; in it you shall not do any work, you, or your son, or your daughter, your manservant, or your maidservant, or your cattle, or the sojourner who is within your gates; ¹¹for in six days the Lord made heaven and earth, the sea, and all that is in them, and rested the seventh day; therefore the Lord blessed the sabbath day and hallowed it.

12 "Honor your father and your mother, that your days may be long in the land which the Lord your God gives you.

13 "You shall not kill.

14 "You shall not commit adultery.

15 "You shall not steal.

16 "You shall not bear false witness against your neighbor.

17 "You shall not covet your neighbor's house; you shall not covet your neighbor's wife, or his manservant, or his maidservant, or his ox, or his ass, or anything that is your neighbor's."

1

The Ten Commandments
in a Day of Grace

We now have the liberating understanding of Galatians 3:19-24 which assures us so forcibly that we have moved from life under law to life under grace. We are able to say with the authority of Ephesians 2:8 and 9: "For by grace you have been saved through faith; and this is not of your own doing, it is the gift of God—not because of works, lest any man should boast."

We can go farther and state that because we are saved the Holy Spirit indwells us and enables us to pursue a higher walk which goes beyond the commands of the Law.

After we have made these points, however, we must ask ourselves what the place of the Ten Commandments can be in our new grace relationship.

Are they obsolete?

Are they merely an echo from a long-ago past?

I believe not.

I believe the Ten Commandments still stand as pillars of direction for the actions of mankind and of governments.

I also treasure the thought that they are loving, helpful signposts which shout to us, "Don't bother to try this type of action.

It won't work! It has not worked in any period of history, and it is still defeating."

Murder creates despair. Thievery creates sadness and shame. Adultery creates problems too broad to be categorized by any one set of terms.

Indeed, the plans of life forbidden by the Ten Commandments will not work if a life of contentment and serenity is the aim.

The Ten Commandments were so important for the lives of Israel that God and the very angels delivered them to Moses in a setting of thunderings and lightning as God wrote with His own hand on pillars of stone.

Since that day, the Law has completed its original task which was to become "our custodian until Christ came, that we might be justified by faith" (Gal. 3:24), but it remains as instruction toward a life of God-honoring love, as well as honesty and cleanness of experience with others.

But here we children of grace are forced to stop and consider, for as believers in Christ we realize that we cannot even obey these laws in our own strength. We must say with Paul that "God is at work in you, both to will and to work for his good pleasure" (Phil. 2:13).

Therefore, both looking backward at that wonderful day when the mountain smoked and Moses' face shown so brightly that it had to be covered by a veil, and at the same time looking forward into our modern day of growth and concurrent questioning of new patterns of life, let us consider again these Ten Commandments. Let us try to see what influence and blessings they can pour upon our lives.

How did they come to us?
What can they teach us?
What is their challenge?
And what is their promise?

2

Unforgettable Events at Sinai

The Law was given to humanity by the voice and hand of God in a series of events more dramatic and powerful than we are able to absorb. The giving was not the act of a moment or a day; it was a divine pageant which occupied many months.

The children of Israel had left Egypt behind and in the third month had come into the wilderness of Sinai where they camped before the great mountain (Ex. 19:1).

As they rested, Moses drew apart, and the Lord called to him out of the mountain, telling him to carry a message back to the people of Israel.

The message was both a reminder of the manner in which God had delivered them from the Egyptians as though they rode "on eagles' wings" and an assurance that He had brought them away from an evil unto Himself.

God made a promise to them with a condition. He promised that if they would obey His voice, they would surely be "my own possession among all peoples . . . a kingdom of priests and a holy nation" (vv. 5-6).

Moses returned, called the elders of the people, and told them the words of the Lord, the people all accepted the charge with a single voice.

Moses, acting as a chosen messenger, carried the words of the people to the Lord and there received the instructions for the future setting for his speaking with all the people. They were to be clean and prepared on the third day when the Lord would come down upon Mount Sinai. The people were not to go up into the mountain or touch its border upon penalty of death. They were to wait for the sound of the trumpet, and when the long sound came, they were to come near.

On the morning of the third day, there was thunder and lightning, and a thick cloud shrouded the mountain. The voice of the trumpet sounded, and Moses brought the trembling people out of the camp to meet with God. They came with awe and stood waiting.

The mountain quaked, and the black smoke hung heavy and curtainlike. The trumpet spoke its announcement, and the Lord came down upon Mount Sinai in fire. From the brightness, He called to Moses to come up to the top of the mountain, bringing Aaron with him (vv. 18-24).

In this awesome setting, God spoke the Ten Commandments in a tremendous voice (20:1).

When the people heard and saw the thunderings and lightning and heard the sound of the trumpet, they moved back in fear and astonishment as they called out to Moses to repeat for them God's words. They pleaded with Moses not to let God speak directly to them for fear they would die.

Moses spoke comfortingly. "Do not fear; for God has come to prove you, and that the fear of him may be before your eyes, that you may not sin" (v. 20).

The Lord again spoke to Moses and commanded him to make an altar of earth where he could sacrifice burnt offerings and peace offerings. He again gave assurances of nearness to Israel, along with a series of commands dealing with the daily life of Israel, justice in all matters, and the laws of the sabbath and the feasts. God further promised the presence of an angel to bring the people to a place He had prepared for them (23:23).

Moses recorded the words and judgments of the Lord and built an altar at the foot of the mountain where he read aloud in the hearing of the people. Around him the voice of the people rose, declaring obedience to God's commands (24:3-4).

Moses, Aaron, Nadab, Abihu, and seventy elders at God's command then went up to worship, and there they saw the beauty of the God of Israel standing as it were on a paved work of clear sapphire (vv. 9-10).

Here it was that Moses received the instructions to come to God to receive the Ten Commandments, now written on tablets of stone, in order that he could teach them to the people from a permanent record (v. 12).

Before departing to receive the Commandments, Moses instructed the people that Aaron and Hur would remain with them as their leaders, and Moses went up onto the mountain where the glory of God rested on Sinai, and a cloud covered the summit for six days.

On the seventh day God called to Moses out of the cloud, and the sight of the glory of the Lord was like an overwhelming, consuming fire. Moses went into the surrounding cloud and remained on the mountain for forty days and forty nights.

There in the midst of the cloud and brilliant fire God spoke at length with Moses, and at the close of this preparation He gave Moses the two tablets of the testimony, tablets of stone, written upon by the finger of God Himself (31:18).

And so the law was given in writing after first being spoken by the voice of God.

The days passed with Moses away on the mountain, and the people below became restless and concerned about his absence. Perhaps he would never return. Who was this Moses anyway? They questioned and complained; then they begged Aaron to make a golden calf to be a god to go before them in the frightening wilderness. And Aaron followed their requests, collecting their golden earrings to mold into the shape they desired. Then he built an altar to the gleaming statue and proclaimed a feast.

On Sinai, God told Moses of the corruption of the people at the foot of the mountain, and Moses pleaded their cause before Him. With a heavy heart as he envisioned what lay before him, and at the same time an awed and triumphant heart as he recalled the hours past, Moses went down, carrying the two tablets of stone (32:19).

His mind was perhaps not prepared for the sight and sound of the wild celebration which greeted him as he approached the camp, and his anger became so fierce that he threw the tablets down and broke them at the foot of Mount Sinai.

His anger still raged against the evil of the people, and he burned the golden calf in the fire and ground it to a bright, hateful powder.

In the calm that followed, Moses viewed the evidence of unrestrained evil and stood in the entrance of the camp and called out to those who were on the Lord's side to come to him. The sons of Levi stepped forward.

God commanded Moses to lead the people away from Sinai toward the land He had prepared for them, and God sent His angel to accompany them for fear He would kill them for their disobedience (33:2-3).

The people camped by Mount Horeb, and the Lord kept a presence near as He spoke with Moses in the tabernacle at the edge of the camp. He spoke face-to-face as a man speaks to his friend while the pillar of cloud stood at the door for all to see.

Moses spoke with God and reasoned that, although God had told him that He knew him by name, he wished to know more of God's way. God assured Moses in comforting words that His Presence would go with him, and that He would give him rest (vv. 12-14).

Moses persisted with God and asked for a sight of His glory in order that he and his people could know that they had found grace in His sight.

In profound love God spoke words of assurance and then explained to Moses that, although no human being could see His face and live, His glory would pass by as He put Moses in the cleft of a rock and covered him with His hand. When He had passed, He would take His hand away, and Moses would see His back.

God then presented a marvelous new command.

He told Moses to cut two tablets of stone like the earlier two on which the Ten Commandments had been inscribed (34:1). The following morning he was to bring the tablets and present himself to God on the top of Mount Sinai.

Moses did as he was commanded. He took the stones and went alone, and the Lord descended in a cloud. Moses remained forty days and forty nights while God instructed him. And again Moses received the Ten Commandments from God, this time written upon the stones Moses had prepared (v. 28).

After the forty days and nights alone with God on the mountain top, Moses again returned to the camp below. But he was not aware that his face shone (v. 29). Aaron and those who waited were afraid to come near Moses, and when he had finished speaking, he covered his face with a veil. In the days that followed he removed the veil as he went into the tabernacle to talk with God, but when he came out to be with the people, he again covered his face because of their dread.

Under the direction of God, Moses ordered the preparation of a permanent resting place for the Ten Commandments (35: 10-12). The ark of the covenant was hewn with skillful care, even as Bezalel (31:2), the chosen artisan of God, designed and worked with the details of furnishings of gold, silver, and jewels, as well as the hangings of fine linen for the tabernacle in which the ark was to rest (Deut. 10:3).

The Law was given.
The resting place was prepared.
God had placed His commands, carved on stone, among His people.

3

Positive Power from the
First Commandment
Choose Me as Your One True God

"You shall have no other gods before me (Ex. 20:3)."

Viewpoint

The First Commandment marks the true beginning for each of us as it writes its message on the world:

Choose Me for the first position in your life.

Choose Me, and Me alone.

Choose Me as your Leader.

As I think of these words I cannot escape a mental picture of a procession, a parade, a glorious march, and that procession must be called *life*. Further, and very personally, that procession must be called *your life* and *my life* because the story of Christianity is one of individuals no wiser or no more foolish than each of us.

As the image of a procession continues, words from the twenty-third Psalm complete a picture of perfect love and care. First, there is God marching as the honored, revered, and perfect Leader. Second, each of us appears, walking confidently behind the One who is total God. In the third position there

19

appears the essence of the psalmist's words which say, "Surely goodness and mercy shall follow me all the days of my life."

And suddenly we see in the procession's formation the diagram of the Christian life: God leads, humans follow, and the blessing of God pursues and protects continually. It is one more picture of God's assurance that everything is cared for. All is in order. But it is mankind which must make the original choice of a leader for the march, even as it is God who makes the issue clear as He speaks in the words of the First Commandment and directs us toward our choice.

Everything begins with a choice!

The very word *choice* may be seen as the theme of our period of history. Never before have so many life choices been open to so many people; they exist on every level of importance.

Do you choose to learn to paint with acrylics? Look in the newspaper for a class scheduled in your area. Do you want to drive a giant truck? Call the number displayed on your television screen. Do you want to take a trip to Alaska? Send for a brochure. Do you want to change professions? Make an appointment with a career counselor. Whatever your choice, not only does it exist, but there is someone available to help you with that choice. But one choice stands apart because of its importance, and that is the one we are considering—the choice of the God who will lead our lives.

Consider the unique value of this choice:

Wherever your leader goes, you go, for this is the essential concept of a leader.

You bear your leader's name, his direction, his aims, his speed of march; in short you become a reproduction of your leader.

Specifically, the choice of a leader is the choice of a pattern for the future.

Can it possibly be that important?

It cannot escape that importance, for wherever the leader

goes, there go the followers, and herein lies the beauty of the First Commandment as the thoughts ring so positively: choose Me as your eternal God, your one true God, your one clear pattern for life.

The implications are beyond number. They instigate all worthwhile action which follows. They are literally the great, good, and positive voice of God telling us to choose perfection in the form of God as our Leader.

This choice is the most noble and awe-inspiring choice ever presented to mankind.

If we place another at the head of life, there is no place remaining for God to fill, for He cannot assume a second rank.

Can you imagine the strangeness of God waiting in the theater wings while another overspreads the stage? Since He created the stage of all the universe, He must occupy His rightful place or leave the tilting dais to its own crumbling fate.

What small deities struggle to occupy God's place! And what surprising movements they make to convince us for a time that they are beautiful, wise, and fulfilling!

"You shall have no other gods before me" (Ex. 20:3).

The human mind loves the reasonable; and this is most reasonable, that He who knows best the created product should direct the development of the uses of that product. Such is the story of God's relationship to the people whom He created.

God claims for Himself the position at the head of that which is His own. And we are His own.

To place other gods where they may block the power of the One who created all is as foolish as to place a shroud before the sun and shiver in the dusky gloom.

"You shall have no other gods before me" (Ex. 20:3).

I have never heard any person say:
  a. I am sorry I studied and learned;
  b. I am sorry I was kind to another;
     or
  c. I am sorry I obeyed God.
I believe there is some deep reality
for life embedded here.

The life of humanity advances both outward and upward, and the leader who charts the way must know the meaning of both paths.

When God says that He must be the first and the total God of life, He is saying that He wishes to surround us with total goodness as we move through our days.

"You shall have no other gods before me" (Ex. 20:3).

Rational human beings can place only God in the station of leadership, for He alone understands the misty, unknown stretches of eternity as well as the restless, urgent schedule of our days. God alone holds the knowledge of all ages in His mind.

God might say to each of us: "Because I am the architect of your life, I am claiming the right to complete My design, to see it stand in undisputed beauty against the noon sky."

Our relationship with God is unique. It was established with infinite care. Never did He consider making us slaves to His plans or subjects of His whims. Always we have had a relationship of honor, trust, and open choice.

"You shall have no other gods before me" (Ex. 20:3).

The Stages of Life

We need not falter in placing God at the front
    of the epochs of humankind.
He knows the meaning of all stages of life.
He knows the meaning of infancy, childhood,
    maturity, and beyond.
He has seen the progression of years
    in numbers of lives beyond the counting.
There are no surprises here for Him.
His hand is sure in guiding each interval
    and each era.

"You shall have no other gods before me" (Ex. 20:3).

A Cry of Wonder at the First Commandment

Did You say we are to place You first in our lives?
Do you mean place your instruction before the conflicting,
    wise words spoken by so many others?
Do You mean place You first before all the books and
    television reports which explain to us that You are
    the God of another age, of another kind of people
    with a different experience of life?
Do You mean place You first in our minds before all the
    interesting things which clamor for our attention?
Do You mean place You first in our time schedules when
    we are already under such pressure to accomplish?
Do You mean place You first before our personal ambition
    and dreams?

I hear Your voice: "Yes." But then You add in apparent
    amazement,
"But why do you assume you will be giving up so many
    good things to place Me first?
The exact opposite is true.
When you place Me first, your understanding will be richer.
    Your learning will be more valid.
    Your hours will be more fulfilled.
    Your dreams will be more beautiful.
Don't you know that I created you with abilities and
    potentials, and I would see them flower into reality?
I have told you to place Me first, and I will lead you into
    the realization of that for which your life is designed!
I know all the answers for all the questions of your mind,
    for I created the substance of all solutions.
Let Me lead you into all the wonders I understand
    completely.
This is My message and the reason for My command."

Balance

The relationship of God and humanity was set
    before recorded time.
He is our Father, and we are His beloved children.
Why should we wish to turn from this mutuality
    which has so blessed human life?
The balance is true.
We are related in a perfect symmetry.

He is the Creator, and we are that which was created;
He is loving spirit, and we are responding beings.
This correlation was established in the ages
    before mankind was reality.
Let it stand.

"You shall have no other gods before me" (Ex. 20:3).

An Exercise for Thought

Recite the name of any god, force, activity, desire,
    or love which could take the place of God in your life.

Count the imposter's days and compare them with God's
    eternity.

Weigh its power and compare that with His strength.

Measure its love and compare that with His compassion.

Then make the choice between God and that which
    intrudes itself into the divine equation which
    God forms with human beings.

"You shall have no other gods before me" (Ex. 20:3).

"It is the Lord who goes before you; he will be with you, he will not fail you or forsake you; do not fear or be dismayed" (Deut. 31:8).

God May Ask

"What more can any leader who walks before you promise
    than that He will be with you,
    He will not abandon you,
    He will not renounce you?
Is there some fear which the human mind carries
    which the mind of God does not know?
If not, why would you fail to trust after I have given
    such assurances?"

"You shall have no other gods before me" (Ex. 20:3).

4

Positive Power from the Second Commandment
Seek to Worship God in Purity

"You shall not make for yourself a graven image" (Ex. 20:4).

Viewpoint

God offers us the openness of a personal relationship with Himself. This is the message of the Second Commandment. We need no intervening presence of objects to complete the relationship—no idols, no carved images, only an unobstructed purity of fellowship.

But how can mankind worship God in purity?

This is a question we can think about for a lifetime, and it is doubtlessly close to God's heart. Further, it is the question which churches, as well as millions of individuals, have faced through the ages.

A part of the answer to the question is expressed in each prayer offered either alone or in a group, in each hymn sung, in each sermon either preached or listened to, and in each private acknowledgment of sin uttered. Each of these experiences represents a step in the aim of pure worship of our perfect God.

The always-deepening answer must be that we worship in the

power of the Holy Spirit through Jesus Christ, since He is our Mediator and the One in whose name we pray. Thus, in Him lies the real purity of worship.

In the Second Commandment, however, we find further details and specific instructions for worship as we are told to avoid images for worship shaped by human hands. We may widen our eyes in surprised disgust at such alien thoughts as golden statues for aids in worship, for how strange such images seem; certainly, idol worship has taken on vastly different forms in our culture.

Bible scholars, in an attempt to discover the attraction of the early Israelites to the ancient forms, have come to the conclusion that the orgies which accompanied idol worship, coupled with the attraction of wealth and luxury which the gleaming gold represented, became a powerful magnet to draw to itself an agricultural people unaccustomed to such display.

But many would say that we have only chosen new idols, and their hypnotic attraction for us would be even more difficult to identify. Our own choices seem to fall more into the category of overpowering fixations, subjects of adoration, or brilliant focuses intruding themselves into our worship, for we remain easily diverted beings in spite of our enhanced way of life.

Even as we view this side of our nature, we hear the Word of God urging us toward purity of worship. We understand without being instructed specifically that the satisfaction of the uncluttered experience of worship can become a reality to each of us. This understanding is doubtlessly the leading of the Holy Spirit toward purer worship.

Exactly how important do we suppose this Commandment is to the mind of God? I am sure we cannot even imagine the answer, but it cannot be escaped that only the command to keep the sabbath day holy exceeds this command in the amount of biblical space devoted to it. Some ninety words are used to expand this thought and make the command more clear.

God tells us that He wants our pure, true, unobstructed worship because He is a jealous God who desires us for His own. This is one of the mighty, truly positive statements of all history! God treasures us! He treasures our worship! He wants a deep, pure relationship of His Spirit with our spirits! He wants no intrusion of imagined heavenly shapes or beings, for none is necessary. True completion of worship has been cared for. As always, we remain able to obey His commands because He has enabled us to do so.

The first four Commandments are concerned with our relationship with God himself. Then follow the commands of our relationship with others. There is no question here of the vibrant movement of human actions outward from the internal source of our relationship, our pure worship of God.

The command to worship God purely is a part of all this positive opportunity to worship freely without obstacles. We need no helps, no carved reminders of who God is. This commandment reaffirms that for us there is an open door welcoming us into new depths of worship of our eternal God.

The face, the hands, the feet of a carved animal could scarcely in any period of time pretend to represent real beauty, much less the beauty of a loving God.

Doubtlessly it is a testimony to the weakness of mankind that people could choose to worship a reproduction of an imagined god over the reality of a perfect God.

Worship is a response of love between two spirits. It cannot ever be completely understood; it can only be reverenced, appreciated, and deeply enjoyed.

"You shall not make for yourself a graven image" (Ex. 20:4).

What can intrude itself between humanity and God as surely as any carved image of worship?

The patterns of life which obstruct, of course.

The endless motions which often fill our days, of course.

And even the strange little guilts and shadows which momentarily call out to us and implore, "Who are you that you would dare approach eternal God?"

The command of God to approach Him in prayer and worship is the kindest of all spoken words, for without this command who would dare approach His throne?

Contentment is a special by-product which is produced in the time of worship.

"You shall not make for yourself a graven image" (Ex. 20:4).

Humans alone could not even guess at methods of worship which would glorify a perfect spirit; therefore, the command to purity of worship without the aid of exterior helps stands as one more evidence of God's provision for His beloved people.

"To whom then will you liken God?
  or what likeness compare with him?" (Isa. 40:18).
In this verse lies the human problem of assisting His worship with outward forms. God is like no other, and His uniqueness cannot be captured except by the heart.

The human heart speaks to God, and worship is complete.

"You shall not make for youself a graven image" (Ex. 20:4).

There is no need for an image created by the human mind to relate the Spirit of our God to the spirit of His own created children.

Whatever we may adore with all our being can threaten to become an idol for us, not graven or carved in stone perhaps, but equally urgent in its call for our worship.

Surely, however, with all the wonderful provisions God has made for our joy, we can savor, treasure, and yet love more than all of these the perfect God who gives us peace and goodness in our lives.

"You shall not make for yourself a graven image" (Ex. 20:4).

The denial of God's law creates its own punishment. God cannot be labeled an avenging spirit where His law is concerned; rather, He stands as a guiding monument directing, always directing, toward that action which creates contentment.

"Worship him who made heaven, and earth, the sea and the fountains of water" (Rev. 14:7).

The angel of Revelation cries out for humanity to give glory to God, and to worship Him who created all. It is our challenge to discover the ways to obey this command in our own lives.

The pure request at dawn for God's hand upon the day is a simple act of worship.

"You shall not make for yourself a graven image" (Ex. 20:4).

From a practical viewpoint, we see that an understanding of strategy directs us to worship purely, without obstruction. Herein lies the clearest communication. He can best direct our walk through life when no intervening element need be consulted.

The mind and heart remain hungry for worship, and when they do not accept the true object of worship, they may, without understanding the choice, worship the emptiness of an image of God.

"You shall not make for yourself a graven image" (Ex. 20:4).

Sometimes we may find it convenient to substitute confusion for pure worship. God brings us back to reality by ordaining the worship of an undefiled, uncomplicated mind and heart.

It goes without saying that a true God cannot receive worship through a screen of untrue images.

To worship an idol which is "like" God, but is not God, can only lead to confusion in the mind of the worshiper.

As the desire to love and please God grows within us, worship itself may automatically shed the falseness which is displeasing to God.

"You shall not make for yourself a graven image" (Ex. 20:4).

God commands that we, whom He loves, not bow down before an idol which is so far beneath His own perfection.

As we now share His very life, through the presence of the Holy Spirit, we realize that this is the cleansing command to bow only before that which is perfect. Further, it is a command to give reverence only to those aims and actions in our own lives which He is constantly shaping for His own purposes.

The divine commands of the Decalogue have molded our civilization. Some appear written in the hearts of untaught people in remote cultures. Others appear in learned legal codes throughout great nations. And all live on and on as universal rules, necessary for the progress of mankind.

"You shall not make for yourself a graven image" (Ex. 20:4).

When God tells us that He is a "jealous" God, He is telling us
not only that He is jealous of our love for Himself but also that
He is jealous of His own plans and design of worship.
He is, in short, jealous for the goodness and freshness of the
worship which He commands—the worship of the loving heart.

God first claims His position as the Head of each life, then He
instructs us to leave every path to Himself unobstructed by
obstacles.

"You shall not make for yourself a graven image" (Ex. 20:4).

We may recall those moments when the voice of God was clearest to us. Then we can return to like circumstances and similar moments as we seek to worship.

The noise and chatter of small events may impede worship as surely as the noise and turbulence of catastrophe.

When people worship, the entire world seems clean.

"God is spirit, and those who worship him must worship in spirit and truth" (John 4:24).
No words can speak more clearly than these of the nature of God; and yet, it is difficult for the human mind to comprehend the meaning of a perfect Spirit who loves and blesses always in spirit and truth.

"You shall not make for yourself a graven image" (Ex. 20:4).

5

Positive Power from the Third Commandment
Give Reverence to God's Name

"You shall not take the name of the Lord your God in vain"
(Ex. 20:7).

Viewpoint

Reverence My name!
Set My identification apart from all others!
Use My name to reveal Who I truly am!

These are instructions deep within God's command regarding His name. But why this heavy emphasis on a mere name? A mere name? No, a name could never be regarded as a "mere name," for that name remains the stamp and identifier of a person throughout all time.

My father-in-law's name was Lee Victor Prokop. No, that was only the name by which he was called—and this is the reason for mentioning what to me is a moving story in reference to a name.

The name on his 1885 birth certificate was Lee Vaclav Prokop, and the family was quick to agree that even the first name appeared as a contraction of a more difficult Old-World name which the attending physician shortened for convenience sake at the time of Lee's birth. And further, the last name when spoken by a native tongue sounded very different from the name as we now pronounce it.

As the young man grew up and began his life's work, his associates could neither pronounce nor remember his difficult name, and it became a hindrance to him. For this reason he changed the name to Lee Victor Prokop.

The years passed, and doubtlessly he became familiar with the new name, but apparently something within him never accepted the name as his own. I began to realize how this change of name had affected him when I heard him introduce himself again and again by saying, "They call me Lee Victor Prokop."

He did not say, "My name is Lee Victor Prokop," for indeed it was not. It was only the name by which others called him, and to him the original name was who he was; the other was a title of convenience.

Would you feel that your name had actually changed if others started, for no reason at all, to call you Stephen, Nancy, Jim, or Maggie, when these names were not your own? At best you would feel confused, and at worst you would feel highly resentful. We cannot fail to realize that some type of adjustment would have to be made to a new title, a new name. And here we are speaking only of human names!

How much more would a perfect God, the Creator of all things, treasure His own identification and descriptive title? How little would He be inclined to surrender His very identification to the casual whim of idle conversation, the unrestrained shout of anger, or the scornful reaction to insignificant events? God could not accept such disrespect! His word says that He will not accept it, for we find in this command, "For the Lord will not hold him guiltless who takes his name in vain" (Ex. 20:7). His name is perfect, and that name must remain without distortion before the world.

The thought of distortion of His name is basic to this command. God stands for all that is great and good, and His name is an instant testimony of these characteristics. We see readily that a denial of His greatness by scorn or dishonesty is the instant result of misuse of His name. The two concepts of name and essence simply cannot be separated, for they are too deeply entwined.

The psalmist speaks of those who give glory to God's name. Again, there are references to His name as a place of safety, a strong tower, where there is refuge. Isaiah 42:8 speaks perhaps the strongest word regarding the significance of a name as God identifies Himself, "I am the Lord, that is my name; my glory I give to no another."

People have always used God's name as the deepest guarantee for vows and covenants, and this system has remained for legal purposes to the present. However, when false swearing occurs, God cannot be honored, and many think that this command against the misuse of God's name in such legal matters is a large part of the biblical background of this command. Certainly, it must be seen as a part of that heritage, but also the fact cannot be escaped that on the level of daily living, deep respect for God's name must prohibit its use for idle exclamations and profane references, as well as for dishonest vows.

In the final analysis, we cannot escape the fact that the command is a positive aid to worship in our individual lives. It is one other word of instruction which serves to clarify for us what kind of God we worship. He is, in fact, Lord, and He is identified as such. He is God! And He tells us that this is His name.

We seek for beauty all of our lives, and this is good. It is an evidence that there is something within us which reaches out toward perfection, the perfection such as we know rests in the being and name of God.

Our minds respond instantly to those family names which represent the beginnings, roots, and strengths of our country. How much more do our minds respond to the family relationship which we bear through God's name.

To honor is to celebrate, and the word *celebrate* carries the thought of happiness. Whether we honor a day or honor the name of our God, the thought remains true. Happiness is the experienced emotion.

"You shall not take the name of the Lord your God in vain" (Ex. 20:7).

Since the first four Commandments speak of worship, we see
that the Commandment to reverence God's name is a part of
worship itself.

"I am the Lord your God" (Ex. 20:2). These are the words with
which God introduced Himself as He began to speak the Ten
Commandments.
The emphasis He placed on His own name and identification
in this highly significant moment tells us of the reverence for
His name which He anticipates receiving from us, His people.

God has exalted Jesus by giving Him "the name which is above
every name" (Phil. 2:9). Herein is an understanding of the love
and reverence which exists within the Trinity.

"You shall not take the name of the Lord your God in vain"
(Ex. 20:7).

"This is my name for ever, and thus I am to be remembered to all generations" (Ex. 3:15c).

A name is a title, a banner, a designation, and an identification. Is it any wonder that God holds His name apart to serve as the word which speaks of perfection?

"Say this to the people of Israel, "I AM has sent me to you" (Ex. 3:14b).

God spoke His own name as "I AM," a name too inclusive to be comprehended by humans. He is all and above all, and we can only grant with love that His name supercedes all other names.

God could not share His name with another, for He cannot divide His being with another.

"You shall not take the name of the Lord your God in vain" (Ex. 20:7).

A name serves as a symbol of all the acts done by its holder. It is the sign under which each act is done, and only goodness moves under the symbol of God.

A name of joy, of hope, and salvation cannot be reduced to casual, thoughtless speaking.

Eternity is charted in length by the time which His name will be remembered. Such is the exactness of His name.

"For my name is in him" (Ex. 23:21).
He speaks of placing His name within us. Because of this principle, mankind gains a new dignity.

"You shall not take the name of the Lord your God in vain" (Ex. 20:7).

His name is a word to be set aside in our minds to bring instant stability. It reminds us that He still is, and that He still rules in this, His world.

Each of us walks beneath some banner which is so easily read by others.

It is only the bearers who fool themselves into believing the banner is obscure or difficult to read.

The selection of a banner bearing God's name is the selection of both life eternal and a very present way of life.

God's name is the name of all our hope and our confidence in every prayer we pray.

"You shall not take the name of the Lord your God in vain" (Ex. 20:7).

The names of God are both too great and too numerous to be listed completely. Each reveals some new aspect of God's provision for His people.

I AM   *Exodus 3:14*
Almighty God   *Genesis 17:1*
El Shaddai   *Genesis 17:1*
Jehovah   *Exodus 34:6*
Jehovah Elohim   *Exodus 34:6*
Jehovah-shalom   *Exodus 34:6*
Jehovah Sabaoth   *1 Samuel 1:3*
Lord of Hosts   *1 Samuel 1:3*
Most High   *Genesis 14:18*
Jehovah-jireh   *Exodus 34:6*

Where else have such terms been amassed to identify a single being?

Where else in history have such titles accompanied a single name?

"You shall not take the name of the Lord your God in vain" (Ex. 20:7).

The psalmist tells us that only God's Word is magnified above His name, for such is the value, strength, and beauty of the name which tells who He truly is (Ps. 138:2).

Blessing brings contentment and joy—and blessing as surely follows the giving of respect to God's name as any other act of worship.

God's name, even as other names, is spoken as human beings call out for communication with its Owner; therefore, it is the name used in prayer.

A name is the summation of all that is within a being, whether that name is the title of God or a person.

Each person creates the meaning of his own name as he decides the kind of person he will be. God created His name as a title for love.

"You shall not take the name of the Lord your God in vain" (Ex. 20:7).

His name was called Wonderful, Counselor, the Mighty God,
The Everlasting Father, and the Prince of peace before His
birth. What greater words can be added, and what lesser words
would anyone wish to use to speak of Him?

"Do everything in the name of the Lord Jesus" (Col. 3:17).
These words paint in with firm brush strokes the motivation for
all actions. They state positively that in God's sight there is a
reason for the pursuit of honor and goodness—the reason is
that we move always in the name of another. That one is God.

God's people pray in the power of His name, act in the strength
of His name, and find their peace in the shadow of His name;
such are the dimensions of His name.

"You shall not take the name of the Lord your God in vain"
(Ex. 20:7).

6

Positive Power from the Fourth Commandment
Set God's Day of Worship and Rest Apart

"Remember the sabbath day, to keep it holy" (Ex. 20:4).

Viewpoint

The Christian happily begins his look at the Fourth Commandment with Matthew 12:8 which places the sabbath in proper perspective. "For the Son of Man is Lord even of the Sabbath," Jesus said, and indeed His view of the day was far different from that of the Jews.

Not only was and is Jesus the Lord even of the sabbath, but He is also the Lord who provides a different and unique rest for His people, the constant rest of the believer in Himself. Thus, differences begin to emerge in the Jewish sabbath and the Christian day of rest. One of the most notable is that of the change from the celebration of Saturday as the day of completed creation to the celebration of Sunday in remembrance of the resurrection.

Changes have come about not only in the day itself but also in the strict rules for the day, yet some things remain the same on a very practical level. For example, we accept with joy the thought of a given day set apart for the special purpose of remembering God and His goodness, and we also accept with special appreciation the remembrance that we need a special day for rest and energizing our own minds, spirits, and bodies. Both of these aims for the day are a part of God's provision for blessing us by showing us a plan for a balanced life. "Remember" and "keep," "work" and "rest"—God knows so well our needs, and He is caring for those needs in this command.

From the earliest beginnings of Genesis 2, we find God setting a day aside for rest at the completion of His creative work. From this example we may well consider that there must indeed be a need within us to stop, rest, reflect, and look beyond the completed tasks of the past to the eternal future. Further, there must be a need to set time apart to think specifically of God and His work.

It cannot be ignored that some of the earliest communications of the Bible deal with this principle of drawing aside to wait quietly and to consider. This is an act of evaluating, rejuvenating, and rekindling which is almost lost in our active, raucous age. But the command remains, waiting to add blessing, contentment, and even strength and youth, for these are some of the characteristics of people who are rested and at ease in their lives.

But how do we satisfy the need for the "rest" of which God speaks? How do we obey the command from God to "remember" and "keep" one day separate from the others?

First, I believe we must constantly refer back to the thought that the Christian's true rest is the rest of Hebrews 4:3: "For we who have believed do enter that rest, as he has said," and this is the rest which might also be called trust. But even as we look at these words we see the helpfulness of the instruction reminding us that a part of our energies and talents, as well as our time, is to be given back to our God in thanksgiving and worship. We trust, and we receive the unique rest which He alone can provide. At the same time we see that we need the drawing apart in remembrance if we are to experience His provision of rest.

Few of us could agree on a totally desirable pattern for the day of rest, and this condition is probably good rather than bad since rest for each of us must be that which satisfies our individual needs for worship and thought.

A startling example of what can develop if the law of God is compressed into a system of minute rules is seen in the teachers of the law spending generation after generation listing those acts which could and could not be performed on the sabbath.

To tie a knot on the sabbath was to work, which was illegal, but first a knot had to be defined. Was the knot which was tied to the handle of a water bucket a violation of the law? Perhaps not, if the knot could be tied with one hand, for that was acceptable, or perhaps if it could be tied to a woman's cap or her girdle, and then in turn to the bucket, for knots holding a woman's clothing in place were permitted. But then, what of untying the knot? Was that a violation of the law as surely as tying the knot in the first place?

The considerations become endless if rules are made for each act, and often the requirements become strangely distorted even with the best of intentions. Who can forget Jesus' being reprimanded for healing on the sabbath? And more important, who can forget His already-quoted answer that He was indeed the Lord of the sabbath.

Too quickly, the rules surpass the spirit of the day, but to ignore the true intent weakens each of us as surely as the overattention to the rules weakened the devout Jews.

Brian and Janie Grassley, who minister in Richland, Washington, came back from a trip to Israel with a new awareness of the special day of rest and remembrance, even though there were basic differences in understanding. Brian wrote:

"During our trip to Israel, one of our lasting impressions came while in Jerusalem during the Jewish Sabbath. On Friday afternoon there was a flurry of activity, then suddenly at sunset it seemed that everything stopped. From sunset Friday until sunset Saturday, the stores were closed, there were very few cars on the street, and all was quiet. During the day on Saturday we observed families taking leisurely strolls in the parks. Saturday evening there was a festive feeling as people filled the streets to talk and share an ice cream cone.

"Janie and I very much appreciated being in an environment that encouraged us to rest and reflect about our Lord. We have made an effort to have a weekly day of rest in our lives since our experience in Israel."

In comments later, Brian went on to tell of the personal enrichment their new view of a day of rest had brought to them. He spoke of Sunday becoming a time when they looked back over the past week to discuss what they had actually accomplished. They analyzed what had been of value and what was mere busy work. They had come to the activity of evaluation anew, but how deeply biblical it was. That first sabbath of the Lord was used by God to contemplate His finished works of creation. He rested and looked back, and "God saw everything that he had made, and, behold, it was very good" (Gen. 1:31a).

Brian also pointed out that the day of rest had become their day of planning for the coming week. I could not keep from wondering what individual or family life would not be enriched by such a plan of giving time specifically to the direction of the future. In this connection, my mind would not let go of the problems of so many troubled marriages which are harried by a couple's inability to communicate their hopes and plans to each other. A shared day could perhaps bring them the stability of seeing their lives develop together. Maybe at least a part of the solution to personal unrest lies in this command written so long ago. Surely we all need time to evaluate the hurried bits of life; we need the time to consider life as a whole—and these are only the human aspects of the command to set a day apart. Beyond these considerations lies the whole world of setting aside one day in seven for worship and remembrance of past love expressed by the Lord.

The Fourth Commandment is basically a command for worship and rest in the Lord, but these are in reality powerful words indicating our need for a life characterized by worship, trust, rest, and remembrance.

Again, in this command, we find the goodness of God offering the happy, totally satisfying life to His children.

In the earliest cuneiform tablets, the sabbath is described as a day of rest for the soul. This thought for a day of worship is definitely hard to surpass.

The day of rest lies like a splendor of peace at the end of the avenue of labor.

"There remains a sabbath rest for the people of God; for whoever enters God's rest also ceases from his labors as God did from his" (Heb. 4:9-10).
God's promise to us is the promise of rest of the spirit, and this is the rest to be most eagerly sought.
This is the rest which keeps the heart contented on the rainiest day.

"Remember the sabbath day, to keep it holy" (Ex. 20:8).

"For in six days the Lord made heaven and earth, the sea, and all that is in them, and rested the seventh day; therefore the Lord blessed the sabbath day and hallowed it" (Ex. 20:11). The day of rest was designed for a memorial to the creation; it remains as a hallowed, set-apart day in which all people may remember the original creation and also take stock of their own efforts at creative work.

In the simplest of terms, God has said to each of us, "Take time to lay aside your regular tasks and think of Me," and in obedience we each find a new dimension of life.

"Remember the sabbath day, to keep it holy" (Ex. 20:8).

God commands us both to labor and to rest. He knows well the secret of the good life for His children.

"You have despised my holy things and profaned my sabbaths" (Ezek. 22:8).
There is something uniquely personal in the way God speaks of His sabbath. Such a special statement of ownership is undoubtedly a reminder of the great importance in His mind and ours of the meaning of a special day of remembrance and rest.

Work is for the developing, advancing, and strengthening of the human mind and muscle; rest is for the deepening and heightening of the mind and spirit.

"Remember the sabbath day, to keep it holy" (Ex. 20:8).

Rest is a pause to evaluate where life and thought have progressed during the past six days.

Work makes its own demands by the practical needs for food and shelter, but the more subtle need for rest may go unheeded.

"You shall keep my sabbaths and reverence my sanctuary: I am the Lord" (Lev. 19:30).
God's nature has not changed from the earliest words of Genesis to the last words of Revelation. Without variation, He demands our reverence, for He is God.

Stress comes when the body is overly tired from the effort toward accomplishment, but stress also comes when the mind carries frustration from too little effort toward the goal.

"Remember the sabbath day, to keep it holy" (Ex. 20:8).

Truly amazing blessings are promised for the one who delights
in fellowship with God on His day. And so significant is this
promise to the mind of God that He concludes it with a reminder that it is He Himself who has spoken.

If you turn back your foot from the sabbath,
     from doing your pleasure on my holy day,
and call the sabbath a delight
     and the holy day of the Lord honorable;
if you honor it, not going your own ways,
     or seeking your own pleasure, or talking idly;
then you shall take delight in the Lord,
     and I will make you ride upon the heights of the earth;
I will feed you with the heritage of Jacob your father,
     for the mouth of the Lord has spoken (Isa. 58:13-14).

"Remember the sabbath day, to keep it holy" (Ex. 20:8).

"Therefore let no one pass judgment on you in questions of food and drink or with regard to a festival or a new moon or a sabbath" (Col. 2:16).

Here the freedom of Christianity is displayed vividly. The commands of God are to the heart of the believer, and the details of regulations fall by the wayside as His grace and love appear. "Love and honor Me totally," God seems to say, "and let the minute legal tangles be a thing of the past."

"Thus saith the Lord; Take heed for the sake of your lives, and do not bear a burden on the sabbath day" (Jer. 17:21).

How wonderful it is when we can understand this as the bearing of mental burdens and recognize that God's plan is that He will bear the burdens for us, on every day of the week. "Casting all your anxieties on him, for he cares about you" (1 Pet. 5:7).

"Remember the sabbath day, to keep it holy" (Ex. 20:8).

God's rest is the quiet flow of constant renewal, but each must seek to find the source of the rest, for the exhilaration of finding His rest is a part of our worship of the Lord who gives all good things to each of us. He has told us, "Therefore, while the promise of entering his rest remains, let us fear lest any of you be judged to have failed to reach it" (Heb. 4:1).

A place of rest is known to the peaceful mind, but the angry mind seeks endlessly for an island of calm.

"This is the rest wherewith ye may cause the weary to rest; and this is the refreshing" (Isa. 28:12, KJV).
Where the Lord dwells, there is rest. The mind knows this fact, but it needs a fresh and constant reminder. Our gift to each other is the reminding.

"Remember the sabbath day, to keep it holy" (Ex. 20:8).

God's rest is a rest even in the day of trouble. It is a rest in spite of surrounding battle.
"And I trembled in myself, that I might rest in the day of trouble" (Hab. 3:16b).

Two words of command He speaks with equal emphasis. "Six days you shall labor and do all your work; But the seventh day is a sabbath to the Lord your God" (Ex. 20:9-10a).
Here is a command for both work and rest, and here lies the equipoise of eternal wisdom, the eternal completeness which brings fulfillment. The dual command holds the balance for the two glories of life, that of work and that of rest.

"Remember the sabbath day, to keep it holy" (Ex. 20:8)

A day of rest provides time for thoughts and remembrance of what was done at Calvary.

The first four Commandments present a listing of steps to understanding our relationship with God in worship. We are made freshly aware of His being, His worship, His name, and His day. Then follows logically our relationship with our fellow human beings.

"Be still before the Lord, and wait patiently for him" (Ps. 37:7). The only perfect rest is that which is found in God's presence. This is the rest of which the Bible most often speaks.

"Remember the sabbath day, to keep it holy" (Ex. 20:8).

"Remember that you were a servant in the land of Egypt, and that the Lord your God brought you out thence with a mighty hand and an outstretched arm; therefore the Lord your God commanded you to keep the sabbath day" (Deut. 5:15).

Here is given another reason for remembering the sabbath, that reason is for appreciation and thanksgiving.

We cannot escape the realization that God is intensely aware of our attitude of thanksgiving for His past blessings and His care of us. An account which illustrates His awareness is the story of the ten lepers who were healed and the one who returned to thank Him. He asked, "Were not ten cleansed? Where are the nine? Was no one found to return to give praise to God except this foreigner?" (Luke 17:17-18).

The separation of one day in seven was a recognizable identification of the separation of a people for God's purposes.

"Remember the sabbath day, to keep it holy" (Ex. 20:8).

7

Positive Power from the Fifth Commandment
In Love, Honor Your Father and Your Mother

"Honor your father and your mother" (Ex. 20:12).

Viewpoint

This is "the first commandment with promise" (see Eph. 6:2). We have heard this description of the Fifth Commandment since we were children, and the description is true and good. There is no reason for us to pull back from the thought of promised blessing in false modesty as though the blessing had not really been promised to each of us. It has, in fact, been promised, and it is only one more of the provisions God's love has created for us.

Perhaps, however, the assurance is not as unique as we might at first think. The words of Deuteronomy 5:33 remind us that a similar promise exists for obedience to all of God's laws. It says, "You shall walk in all the way which the Lord your God has commanded you, that you may live, and that it may go well with you, and that you may live long in the land which you shall possess." Here is a command and then a promise of blessing for obedience: this is an often-repeated biblical pattern.

In the instruction to honor parents is certainly cradled one of the secrets of happiness in the home. We realize instantly that as children honor their parents, it follows that rational parents respond to being honored with very special love and appreciation for their children.

There are many examples in life in which we are able to participate on both sides of a situation. We may at different times be both a player and an observer of a game. We may be both a performer and a listener in a musical event, and the pattern of family development is such that we are both a child and a parent at different stages of life.

There is something rich and rewarding here, since we have an opportunity to evaulate all the emotions and responses of both sides of the situation.

Honor and rejoice in both roles! This is the situation we would wish with all our hearts to experience, and it is, in fact, the biblical pattern insofar as the family is concerned.

A child who is blessed with wise and loving parents may regard the command to esteem father and mother as an almost unnecessary command. To that child the inclination to honor is second nature since the parents he or she knows are in fact honorable. But what of children who know no such situation? Their outlook is different and will perhaps always be tinged with dark emotion, even when they have outgrown any threat from unloving or unconcerned parents.

While the sad situation of neglect exists, in many cases it is possible that the promise which is a part of this command may be a special provision for this circumstance. There is assurance here that God is aware of the unhappy situation and has provided a particular blessing for the child.

As tragic as this whole problem area may be, and as much as every right-thinking person yearns to see it corrected, we know it may remain for a time; however, it may take on a vastly different coloration as the individual responds to the realization that God has promised children special blessings for honoring the parent who is without honor. Day by day problems may well begin to be seen in a different light. They can be viewed as tests to be handled in God's way with the help of His hand and with His blessing.

This principle is taught throughout the Bible and is applicable not only in this area of parent and child; it is the eternal principle of placing the mind on the reality of life in Christ rather than on the constantly changing events which are often confused and even meaningless.

I have never heard any person claim that this principle of looking beyond the event to the reality of Christ is an easy concept to incorporate into the life, but it is the principle which God teaches us over and over as He reminds us to walk with Him and to place our minds on Him. In Ephesians 5:1-2, He sets the pattern: "Therefore be imitators of God, as beloved children. And walk in love, as Christ loved us and gave himself up for us." In these words He is telling us that our source of peace and contentment is found in Him and that the outward appearances may be exactly that—outward appearances which have no reality.

The psalmist looked at the Commandment for obedience and defined a special result, the blessing of an enlarged heart, (or as some have added an explanatory note) of an enlarged understanding or a heart free from anxiety. He sang in Psalm 119:32, "I will run in the way of thy commandments, when thou shalt enlarge my heart" (KJV). When the heart is enlarged, the life and the mind are enlarged, and herein lies the joy of relaxed, expanded living.

All the Commandments are commands with promise, for at the end of the road of obedience lies God's blessing. What greater goodness and happiness can exist in the life than the assurance of blessing? God tells us that the simple act of obedience creates blessing, and although the thought is not complicated, we often forget its reality. It is well worth our efforts to remind ourselves often that His plans are perfect, and our only task is to learn to walk with awareness of the principles which He teaches us repeatedly.

"Children, obey your parents in the Lord, for this is right. 'Honor thy father and mother' (this is the first commandment with promise), that it may be well with you and that you may live long on the earth" (Eph. 6:1-3).

This command knows no time limit. Both the Old and the New Testaments detail it for our instruction.

But only the New Testament goes on to place the total responsibility where it is shared by parent and child.

"Fathers, do not provoke your children to anger, but bring them up in the discipline and instruction of the Lord" (Eph. 6:4).

"Honor you father and your mother" (Ex. 20:12).

Parents are one of the continuing realities of life. The need of children is to try to appreciate the parent-child relationship, even as they show honor. For the relationship is as deep as life itself. It is, in fact, life.

I have always felt that parents are more closely related to their children emotionally than the children are related to the parents. Perhaps this is because parents remember with deep emotion all the events surrounding the child's miracle of birth while the child accepts these reported remembrances simply as another chapter of family life.

Also, the child's birth is a high point of culmination of life for the parents while to the child it is a launching pad from which he or she will move away into the future.

"Honor your father and your mother" (Ex. 20:12).

To give honor to parents gives perspective to life, for such consideration reverences the ongoingness of life.

There is a chain of life from parent to child, and on to the next generation. The stronger this chain remains, the deeper will be the joy of childhood and the anticipation of maturing richly.

By the manner in which we treat our parents, we each teach our own children how we wish to be treated when we are old.

God chose the image of parent and child to draw a picture of His relationship to us. This fact shows the reality of such a tie within earthly families.

"Honor your father and your mother" (Ex. 20:12).

The granting of honor is a double blessing: it blesses the one who is honored and ennobles the one who is willing to grant honor.

Parents can give to a child only that which they have, whether it is good or bad. And the child who is young and insecure, accepts and turns the variable gifts into strengths or weaknesses according to his own character and abilities. The relationship is seldom smooth throughout all of life, but God's law of respect helps to ease confused times.

The parent is the caretaker of the helpless child, and for this function God grants a measure of appreciation and respect.

"Honor your father and your mother (Ex. 20:12).

Giving honor increases the capacity of the donor to appreciate another, and in so doing one builds a citadel of character. Again, we see God's law blessing all who follow its teaching.

Gifts mean the most to children and to the aged, and withholding any good gift which can be given robs the possible donor's character of generosity.

To honor is to give respect, and respect weaves contentment and peace into the fabric of life.

The parent is a figure of the Lord, and as such, if for no other reason, is deserving of respect.

"Honor your father and your mother" (Ex. 20:12).

Honor must be a two-way street as parents honor children and children honor parents. But if either part of the relationship breaks down, God remains. He does not desert the disoriented home; instead, He urges action far beyond normal responsibility and promises unlimited blessing for that action.

Parents who teach their children the Lord's Word day by day, and hour by hour, have reason to anticipate love and respect in return. But even if this respect should not develop, the parents have the joy of knowing they have obeyed God in the matter.

"You shall teach them diligently to your children, and shall talk of them when you sit in your house, and when you walk by the way, when you lie down, and when you rise" (Deut. 6:7).

"Honor your father and your mother" (Ex. 20:12).

God commanded our children to honor us! What a heavy responsibility this placed upon us to be honorable in every sense of the word.

It is as though we enable our children to obey God's command by making ourselves the kind of people they can indeed honor easily.

In the Proverbs we find this thought embedded in the description of the virtuous wife:

"Her children rise up and call her blessed;
    her husband also, and he praises her:
'Many daughters have done excellently, but
you surpass them all' " (Prov. 31:28-29).

To look back and complain of a lack of blessings from parents is to perpetuate the problem by missing the blessings which thankfulness brings into the life.

"Honor your father and your mother" (Ex. 20:12).

8

Positive Power from the Sixth Commandment

Accept the Gift of Life with Reverence

"You shall not kill" (Ex. 20:13).

Viewpoint

The Sixth Commandment, which is concerned with murder, is often seen as the darkest of the ten since the crime of murder is so heinous. But in reality, life and not death is the issue here: God is commanding us to respect another's life, to live our own lives with dignity, and, in short, to value and treasure life. This is the reason He speaks to us with such force, "Do not destroy life!" and as we may say positively, "Reverence life. It is a gift from God."

Further, in this Commandment, God is teaching us to live in the fullest sense of the word and to understand one of His great principles, which is to appreciate life because He is its only source.

Relish life! Grant others their lives! Cherish life! Understand life! Glory in life! Hold onto life! He seems to shout to us, "I am the Giver of life; there is no other origin; therefore, give My gift its proper recognition. Its creation is My unique act. It cannot be duplicated."

The Bible is a Book of life. Its pages are filled with prescriptions for eternal life, abundant life, and committed life. It is a Book which deals with total life. Both heights and depths of experience are quickly found in its pages. We may consider the uses of life it details.

We think sadly of the misuse of a life such as that of Judas. He used his life for betrayal and participated in murder followed by his own tortured death by suicide. His is the ultimate in the waste of the gift of life.

Then we think of a life like Paul's. He served God with a unique kind of vigor and single-mindedness. It brought him to the point that as his death drew near he gloriously summarized his experience by writing, "I have fought the good fight, I have finished the race, I have kept the faith" (2 Tim. 4:7).

It is Jesus, however, who expands the Sixth Commandment to make it a rule and guide for each of us today. In Matthew 5:21-22, He moves the command to the area of our thinking and our intent toward others. He says, "You have heard that it was said to the men of old, 'You shall not kill; and whoever kills shall be liable to judgment.' But I say to you that everyone who is angry with his brother shall be liable to judgment; whoever insults his brother shall be liable to the council, and whoever says, 'You fool!' shall be liable to hellfire."

Jesus was speaking of destructive acts of anger, scorn, and malice toward others, and His emphasis was on an area we may accept somewhat thoughtlessly. He suggested that the partial destruction of life by whittling away at happiness and contentment is viewed by God as sin. Such a line of thought brings us up short as it reminds us of the standards Jesus sets for us. His standards are not only far higher levels of activity than we at first consider as we read the Sixth Commandment, but they are a different type from those of Exodus 20. Their difference lies in the source from which they spring, and that source is Jesus

Himself and His work of creating a new spirit within us through the power of the Holy Spirit.

There is something deeply valuable to the Christian life here, for what we are seeing is God's plan for each of us to view life as He must view it. We may recall easily that humanity does look on the outward appearances while God looks on the heart, but when Jesus uses the word *murder* to describe our attitudes of fierce anger, we are forced to take another look at our minds.

Human beings may scarcely be aware of the condition of their own hearts, feeling that if they are not driven to acts of outward violence they are doing quite well, but Jesus regards the matter differently. His desire for us, His followers, is that we live a vastly higher life, centered in Him. A command to live a life of love, His love, provides the positive side of the darker command to avoid the act of murder.

"For God made man in his own image" (Gen. 9:6).
God leaves no question in our minds of His reason for granting
respect to human life. It is that human beings are made in the
image of God and are therefore a representation of God Himself.

Someone has said that he wondered what life was until he
discovered that it was *he*. How true this is! Life is what we have
and what we are. It is God's gift of a mind and spirit housed
in a case of flesh. In this case we walk through the days until
the time when our days will be spent in His constant presence.
The challenge is to make the walk worthwhile and the days
pleasing to our Creator.

"You shall not kill" (Ex. 20:13).

In God's early words to Noah, He spoke clearly of His love for life. His love was so great that He declared He would protect it, even to the greatest punishment possible of the one who dared destroy it.

"Whoever sheds the blood of man, by man shall his blood be shed" (Gen. 9:6).

When God created us, He placed in us a drive to fight for life. This is another evidence of God's goodness to us, for without this divine urging we could not escape an overpowering desire to leave this earth to go to live in His presence forever.

Life, the gift of God, mingles with the elements of the earth, and then flows gently back to God.

"You shall not kill" (Ex. 20:13).

"What man is there who desires life,
   and covets many days, that he may enjoy good?
   Depart from evil, and do good;
   seek peace, and pursue it" (Ps. 34:12-14).
You shall not murder!
Reverence life!
Desire life and see good days!
These are all steps toward the fullness of life both for ourselves
and others. They reflect the kind of God we have, one who
wishes for us the good will, beauty, and contentment of life
itself.

"But to set the mind on the Spirit is life and peace" (Rom.
8:6b).
Here a spiritual mind is seen as the essence of life itself. There
is no applause for the life which attempts existence apart from
God.

"You shall not kill" (Ex. 20:13).

"For as the Father has life in himself; so he has granted the Son also to have life in himself" (John 5:26).

True tradition reveals itself here. The Father gives life to the begotten Son, and the Son gives life to each who accepts it. This is a revelation of the concept of true family love, and it cannot be ignored that we are those sons and daughters who are so carefully noted in God's book of family remembrance. Further, it cannot be forgotten that life itself is the listed family inheritance.

"I came that they may have life, and have it abundantly" (John 10:10).

God speaks of abundant life almost casually, and why would He speak otherwise? Every act of His being is abundant beyond anything we can yet know or comprehend.

"You shall not kill" (Ex. 20:13).

Life gains tremendous significance because its source is in God.

Jesus' words of care for the lilies of the field, the fowls of the air, and the sparrow which falls from its nest are ultimate examples of His concern for life on every level.
Here is love expressed in terms of reality; here is the love which knows nothing of murder.

"In him was life, and the life was the light of men" (John 1:4). Life in all its aspects was in Him and is still in Him. It must not be handled wantonly by any person, for it is fashioned of divine fabric.

"You shall not kill" (Ex. 20:13).

Bread is the energy-giver of life. It nourishes and sustains. This is the reason it is the perfect metaphor for Jesus whose being is absorbed into the fiber of our lives and thereby produces the strength by which we can function.

"Thou dost show me the path of life" (Ps. 16:11a).
God shows us not only His respect for life itself, but also for the pattern of life. In the words of the psalm He promises to show us the path our lives should seek to take. A reverence for life, a pattern for life, a guide for life—these are the protections of life which God provides with His own love.

God permits us to make the greatest decision of all. We decide between life and death. We express our respect for life as we choose the eternal life He has provided for each of us.

"You shall not kill" (Ex. 20:13).

To destroy another person's life is too terrible for our minds to comprehend; equally terrible, however, is the destruction of one's own life either by one shattering act or by the constant waste of the purpose for which life was created.

"So that as Christ was raised from the dead by the glory of the Father, we too might walk in newness of life" (Rom. 6:4*b*).

The new life of this verse reverences both God and life itself, for the life described here is the life which flourishes because of God's indwelling presence.

"I have been crucified with Christ; it is no longer I who live, but Christ who lives in me" (Gal. 2:20*a*).

"You shall not kill" (Ex. 20:13).

"You have heard that it was said to the men of old, 'You shall not kill, and whoever kills shall be liable to judgment.' But I say to you that every one who is angry with his brother shall be liable to judgment" (Matt. 5:21-22).

Jesus added anger and malice toward our brother as acts of murder. Perhaps these are murder with a two-edged sword. They may destroy two lives at the same time, the one attacked by anger and the one who carries the anger in the heart.

Life takes on a new dimension when we recall the care God has taken for its details. He must love its every aspect—else why would He have invested so much perfect thought in its creation?

"You shall not kill" (Ex. 20:13).

Far back in antiquity, humans began to chart the passage of time by the sundial and by the flow of water or sand. This is an expression of a highly logical pattern of thought, for always humanity has wished to know how much of this precious life on this earth has passed and how much yet remains to be lived.

The closer human beings stand to God, the greater their reverence for life will be.

Jesus spoke of the new life, the holy life, the separated life, the useful life, the blessed life, the helpful life, to mention only a few. He was the voice of and for life, and His message was always of the potential for service in this life.

"You shall not kill" (Ex. 20:13).

9

Positive Power from the
Seventh Commandment
Seek for Purity in Your Life

"You shall not commit adultry" (Ex. 20:14).

Viewpoint

A strangely sad comment on the state of our culture at the
present time is that the theme of adultery is doubtlessly one of
the primary humor situations for television comedies. This is
particularly strange when it is so easily seen that adultery produces neither comedy nor happiness in life. Exactly the opposite is true, and God has given us a command prohibiting it for
exactly this reason. His loving care of His people does not for
a moment sanction action which destroys homes, marriages,
and every aspect of shared lives.

It is probably far from an accident that in Mark 10:19 Jesus
places the command prohibiting adultery before the command
prohibiting murder. Some explain this surprising placement by
suggesting that reasonable followers of Jesus' teachings would
be as concerned with acts which defile the body as they are with
acts which destroy it.

But what is the bright and positive side of the reason for the
command itself which would seem to spread gloom and doom

on lives in search of sexual excitement? The bright side is indeed far brighter than the dark side is dark, for the true message is one of invitation to relaxed love and contentment with a single marriage partner who understands, loves, and respects the entire concept of faithfulness to home and family.

I love to think of the Old Testament Scriptures in which promises of peace and happiness are developed in the pastoral imagery of a family dwelling in safety and fulfillment under its own vine and fig tree. First Kings 4:25 is one such verse, and we find the same word picture of families resting together at the close of the day at least three times. It is a picture of complete repose which creates much the same emotion as a lambent landscape painting or a twilight seascape.

But how is this a part of God's command of sexual purity? It is simply that God's picture of the deeply treasured life is one which is centered in a home where members of a family love each other and where the strife from outside competitive forces is minimized.

With little fear of contradiction, we could say that the act of physical love is one of the truest acts of life sharing. It is a most personal and private act, and there is no possibility of sharing it with outsiders. This is, doubtlessly, the very reason it is so vulnerable to desecration, for always the most valuable gifts run the greatest risk of being destroyed and devalued.

Contrast the agony of mind the normal person would experience on seeing a piece of worn, stained work clothing being ground into the mud by careless feet with the picture of a beautiful hand-painted silk dress receiving the same treatment. We recoil at the very thought of destroying something uniquely beautiful, and by the same token the twisted mind relishes the destruction of a pure, unsullied relationship.

Millions of words have been used to describe the entire area of sexual purity, but it remains that God's Word says it best and most simply. The joy of life and of good days lies in the love of two people, and two alone, the Bible tells us. From the early words of Genesis 2:24 we hear God saying, "Therefore a man leaves his father and his mother and cleaves to his wife, and they become one flesh." Almost as noteworthy as these words themselves is the realization that they appear not as some late development of doctrine but simply as the way God planned for His people to live from the very beginning. We are indeed considering thoughts close to the creative heart of God as we contemplate the Seventh Commandment.

As such, the bond between man and woman can be seen as a relationship which creates peace and happiness privately, and at the same time it becomes a tie which can be evidenced before the world with pride, for it is both right and good.

The picture of a bride in her white dress remains the idealized picture of flawless beauty in the American mind, and may it always be so, for it is the outworking of God's ideal as represented by His command. It says to us, "This is the way of purity and beauty. This way works for happiness and contentment." How carefully God designed us, and then designed the rules which would shape our lives toward richness. He wishes for us long days of contentment with the one we love, and He therefore can approve of no other life-style.

One of my favorite stories is of a friend who rushed to downtown Houston for an urgent business appointment. Running late, he drove from one parking lot to another only to find the inevitable sign, "Parking lot full. No admittance." He drove on until suddenly—Excelsior! There, up an alley behind a department store was an empty space, angled just right to accommodate easy parking! He whirled in, facing the brick wall of the back entrance to the store, and there in giant letters he read, "Don't even think of parking here!"

We chuckled over this well-put warning, but this is the background phrase of each of the Commandments. They shout to us, "Don't even think of trying this action. It can only produce unhappiness! Forget it! Move on to contentment and joy!"

This is the message of the Seventh Commandment.

"You shall not commit adultery" (Ex. 20:14).

Physical and mental strength flourish outwardly from the base of a relaxed, happy household. Such a household has its roots firmly anchored in the Seventh Commandment.

God loves us, and when He speaks a word of command, it is for our own good, our contentment, and our growth. Be loyal to your family and home, He implies, and the thought follows: this is the way of peace and joy for His children.

"At that time, says the Lord, I will be the God of all the families of Israel, and they shall be my people" (Jer. 31:1).
The families of Israel are seen as God's treasures. We have no reason to think that the relationship of God to our own families has changed in any way.

"You shall not commit adultery" (Ex. 20:14).

The Bible is a book of families. We learn of a Heavenly Father whom we worship and a Heavenly Son whom we accept as Savior.

We learn of an ancient prophet, Hosea, redeeming a faithless wife, Gomer, and of a loving king, David, weeping for a disloyal son, Absalom. We learn of Jesus with His last words of care for His own mother, and of Mary and Martha mourning for their brother, Lazarus.

We feel the depth of ties in God's words, and we can come to know that the family is God's plan for His people as they walk through the days of this life.

Accomplishment, whether for God's purposes or for our own need and satisfaction, is most vigorous when it is nurtured by a source of stable homelife.

"You shall not commit adultery" (Ex. 20:14).

Paul erases the last doubt of the source of any uncleanliness in the mind. God is not its author; He has no part in its source. He is pure and therefore He can only create purity in the minds of His people.

"Now the works of the flesh are plain: fornication, impurity, licentiousness" (Gal. 5:19).

"Owe no one anything, except to love one another; for he who loves his neighbor has fulfilled the law" (Rom. 13:8).

An understanding of the purity of love erases the need to ponder for long all undersirable actions, for the outworking of love is goodness, honesty, and concern for others in every circumstance.

"You shall not commit adultery" (Ex. 20:14).

"For out of the heart come evil thoughts, murder, adultery, fornication, theft, false witness, slander. These are what defile a man" (Matt. 15:19-20).

Always Jesus reaches beyond actions to their roots, and in so doing He directs us not only toward purity of action but, much more, to purity of thinking.

Herein lies the very core of Christianity, for all of God's rules begin with the human heart and mind and then work outward to our actions.

Deep respect for the person to whom we are committed is the cornerstone of a loyal relationship.

"You shall not commit adultery" (Ex. 20:14).

A loving home is one of the most beautiful of God's creations, and He expresses His deep concern for it in His Commandment for purity.

"For this reason I bow my knees before the Father, from whom every family in heaven and on earth is named" (Eph. 3:14-15). The family of believers carries a very special name which is the name of our Savior. We are, in fact, known as Christians, thus indicating that we follow the teachings of Christ.

As such, we bear a family name of purity.

What name could possibly imply a higher level of both thought and action?

"You shall not commit adultery" (Ex. 20:14).

10

Positive Power from the Eighth Commandment
Respect All Others' Property Rights

"You shall not steal" (Ex. 20:15).

Viewpoint

Scriptures immediately come to mind in which God forbids us to rob ourselves by overspending, or to rob others by removing the old landmarks. God forbids unlawfully taking from another's vineyard or field, pressing for undue advantage in bargaining, failing to restore what is borrowed or found, or failing to pay debts or wages to employees, as well as withholding from God Himself. Such wide attention to the matter of theft can only indicate that God attaches far-reaching importance to this principle of honesty in all its varied facets.

The positive view of the command against theft forces us to see that the principle is designed for the welfare of all who live around us and for our own benefit as well. God is telling us, "The good life for My people is found in honesty and truth. Honesty and respect for another's property are building blocks for community peace and individual peace of mind."

Property is not God's primary area of interest. We recall quickly His words on the importance of accumulating our treasures in heaven rather than on earth, and He emphasizes else-where that wealth is not the source of contentment, nor is it a reason for self-congratulation. Notwithstanding, He gives property full recognition as both a necessity and as a rightful reward of labor. It cannot be ignored that the ideal woman of Proverbs 31 is applauded for skill and trustworthiness in acquiring warm clothing for her family and for making wise decisions in buying a field. It also would be hard to forget the teachings of Psalms and Proverbs concerning sloth in business.

All of these facts are pivotal because considered together they give us God's perspective of the way our lives can function most effectively; in short, they reveal another part of God's plan for us. We can rightly deduce that property, its acquisition and protection from thieves, is a valid and reasonable part of life. If the would-be thief were willing to assume his responsibility in the matter of property, the problems of the world would be lessened indeed.

There is an old, time-tested guide for making decisions about some matters, and it consists of thinking back to what we have heard people say they were glad or sorry they had done in the past. For example, I have never heard a man say he was glad he had denied help to his children or friends when he could have afforded assistance for them. Also, I have never heard a woman say she was glad she had not given her family the best care she was capable of providing them.

Perhaps such statements have been made, but I have never heard them personally, and this leads me to ask myself whether I have ever heard people say they were pleased that they had taken property which undeniably belonged to another. No, I have never heard it. I can assume generally that theft has not been a satisfying experience for many people; therefore, it is not worth pursuing, especially when the agony of the one robbed is considered.

God has given us a head start on this decision by forbidding theft in all its forms, and common sense adds its reminder that there is no joy in the activity.

We have been thinking in terms of the human right to own property and also the poor investment in life satisfaction which the thief himself makes. But there is a more subtle form of thievery to which each of us may relate on a personal basis. Galatians 6:10 illustrates this principle as it declares: "So then, as we have opportunity, let us do good to all men, and especially to those who are of the household of faith." We may assume that failing to do good to those around us is a violation of the intent of this verse. We might even admit it is an example of stealing goodness, whether it is enjoyment or necessities which we withhold when we are, in fact, in a position to provide them for others.

This is a command to expand, to increase, and to bless the lives of family and friends when the opportunity to do so exists. It is the positive expression of the command not to lessen another's life in any way. The mere lessening is a form of life theft when viewed through God's commands. "Do good" is God's way, and each of us could add that the doing of His way blesses two: the one to whom goodness is done and the one who has been able to do some act of goodness for another.

God's plan of life is complete and full. And only when we step aside from its abundance into close-handed taking of life's joys from others does God's planned life becomes inaccessible to us. "You shall not steal," He commanded so long ago. Paul added a positive word: "Do good," and we can only add an echo from our own experiences of life: do good for others in any way possible, defrauding no one, and herein lies a plan for living richly at peace with God's plans and His very Spirit.

God addresses honesty and its opposite on every level. He describes dishonesty which is directed toward the worker who in turn accuses an unjust employer and finds the help of God waiting (see Prov. 22:22-23). Also, He tells of the dishonesty of those who rob God Himself, as in Malachi 3:8. This says a great deal about the significance of honesty in God's accounting of human affairs.

There is a goodness in the developing and caring for of property, for it speaks of provision for homes and families.

Civilization itself grinds to a halt when people cannot hold their own belongings against thieves. God is recognizing this fact when He urges honesty, for His work flourishes best where people are sufficiently free of chores of property protection to live fruitful lives in His service.

"You shall not steal" (Ex. 20:15).

" 'Has this house, which is called by my name, become a den
of robbers in your eyes? Behold, I myself have seen it,' says the
Lord" (Jer. 7:11).

God is aware of our level of honesty and is quick to cry out
against unbecoming acts. He tells us that He both sees and
notes. What could remind us more forcibly of His view of our
actions?

"Is not my word like fire? says the Lord; and like a hammer
which breaks the rock in pieces? Therefore, behold, I am
against the prophets, says the Lord, who steal my words from
one another" (Jer. 23:29-30).

God speaks with particular vehemence against the prophets
who distort His words, and as He speaks we see the breadth of
the command to deal honestly in every area of life.

"You shall not steal" (Ex. 20:15).

"Therefore, brethren, pick out from among you seven men of good repute full of the Spirit and of wisdom, whom we may appoint to this duty" (Acts 6:3).

We seem automatically to seek out those who are of "good repute" to care for our business. It is not surprising that the early church followed the same plan, for there is a deep need for honor within us not only for practical reasons but also because of some basic respect we share for honorable action.

There is strength in the applause of one person for another's belongings. It is the strength of selflessness which can grant to another the right to achieve surroundings of beauty and contentment.

"You shall not steal" (Ex. 20:15).

"Behold, the money which we found in the mouth of our sacks, we brought back to you from the land of Canaan; how then should we steal silver or gold from your lord's house?" (Gen. 44:8).

There seems never to have been a time in history when men were not aware that it was inappropriate to take property which belonged to another. As early as the verses of Genesis 44 we find lively discussion of intrigue in the area of property theft.

The heart of the thief is the problem, for the thieving heart is a bitter, grasping heart which has no understanding of the wholesome structure of life.

There are vast differences in the types of properties which we each hold, but whether they be necessary objects or moments of joy, they are not available for the marauder's hand.

"You shall not steal" (Ex. 20:15).

"Finally, brethren, whatever is true, whatever is honorable, whatever is pure, whatever is lovely, whatever is gracious, if there is any excellence, if there is anything worthy of praise, think about these things" (Phil. 4:8).

What can be the value of thinking of justice, as well as other commendable virtues? Isn't this a rather strange bit of advice from the mind of God? I think not, because unfailingly we move toward those things which we think about and dwell on. And eventually, probably without our realizing it, they become a part of our beings.

Stealage is an appropriate and usable word from the dictionary. It may surprise us a bit that stealing is so common it has developed a pertinent vocabulary of its own.

"You shall not steal" (Ex. 20:15).

"The thief comes only to steal and kill and destroy; I came that they may have life, and have it abundantly" (John 10:10).

Jesus' words present the contrast between the One who gives perfect gifts and the one who takes away gifts. We find here the positive two-sided mirror of ownership, and hopefully we see ourselves looking back from that side which reflects honesty toward others, along with a deep concern for their well-being.

We need to honor that which is our own, for God is the Source of those things which nourish us. We need also to extend the honor of ownership to others, for they too have received the goodness of gifts from God.

"You shall not steal" (Ex. 20:15).

The very thought of theft is surrounded by words such as *dark, sneak, dishonest, secret,* and *fear.* Such suggestive words alone are enough to cause us to consider what there is to be gained by an act of theft.

God directs us toward total honesty. Can you imagine life if this command were different and spoke only of partial honesty?

Dealing honestly is no more a once-and-for-always action of life than is loving or serving. The whole area must be looked at again and again to be sure dishonesty is not gaining a foothold where we are totally unaware of its movement.

Thieves diminish themselves by reducing their own beings to the level of a despised thing, and they diminish the owners by taking their tranquility from them.

"You shall not steal" (Ex. 20:15).

11

Positive Power from the Ninth Commandment
Speak Truthfully When You Deal with Others' Lives

"You shall not bear false witness against your neighbor" (Ex. 20:16).

Viewpoint

Perhaps one reason for the forceful and unbending negative tone of the Ten Commandments which state so forcefully, "You shall not," is that God was urgently denouncing the evils He saw before Him even in Moses' day. Certainly swearing to a false statement appears again and again in both the Old and the New Testaments; in fact, the corruption appears almost as a continuous thread through the court systems of Bible days.

The New Testament account of Stephen is a story of people being suborned to swear falsely that this man, who was in fact "full of grace and power," was speaking blasphemy. We go on to learn in the details of Acts 6 that Stephen defended himself with such clarity and precision that only additional false witnesses could make the charge against him stick. In verse 15 we read that he stood before them, and they saw his face "as the face of an angel." Yet the witnesses could not be swayed. The contrast between the appearance of the condemned and those who destroyed him with deceit is so glaring that the rational mind can only wish to be in the presence of the accused rather than with the victors.

But further, perhaps as God wrote on stone the command against destruction of other people's character, to say nothing of their very lives, He was looking down the corridors of time to the day His own Son would be tried, convicted, and sentenced to the cross by the words of false swearers. In Matthew 26:59-61 we read. "Now the chief priests and the whole council sought false testimony against Jesus that they might put him to death, but they found none, though many false witnesses came forward. At last two came forward and said, 'This fellow said, "I am able to destroy the temple of God and to build it in three days." ' "

We find similar words in Luke as Jesus stood before Pilate, and the false witnesses brought their empty accusations. As I have studied this command I have felt something deeply personal in God's words. Perhaps it is because it was a part of the dark days of Jesus' trials that the breaking of this Ninth Commandment remains so poignant and affecting to each of us.

Close at hand, we see the more common, more intimate results of false witnesses' words. Their ugliness and destruction are nowhere more clearly addressed than in the thoughts of the commentator Matthew Henry who spoke of the everyday inclination toward slander, backbiting, and tale-bearing, as well as simply making events worse than they are. He spoke of the motive which lurks behind such slander and saw such attacks as an endeavor to raise one's own reputation upon the ruin of a neighbor's.

But even as we consider these words we see that it requires only the shifting of point of view to remind ourselves that the acceptance of honesty and appreciation of others replaces the poverty of such attacks with the richness of honest appreciation.

The beauty of life emerges in the clear, positive teaching that the good, growth-oriented life lies not in the attack but in the defense of others. God's view is one of love, and love speaks of lifting up, never of putting down.

God anointed His creation with resplendent grandeur when He declared that human beings were created in His own image. People can participate in this grandeur as they continue to elevate their own lives by faith and that of their neighbors by encouragement and kindness.

The pages of the Bible remind us to speak justly of other people both behind closed doors and in open court. Such speaking pleases God and brings happiness to people.

Truth can be elusive. Too often it hides without our thinking of it, and the spoken words seem to assume a life of their own.

"You shall not bear false witness against your neighbor" (Ex. 20:16).

"For we have found this man a pestilent fellow, an agitator among all the Jews throughout the world, and a ringleader of the sect of the Nazarenes. He even tried to profane the temple, but we seized him" (Acts 24:5-6).

The false accusations against Paul are indeed unrestrained and rash. Perhaps this is a characteristic of untruth; it tends to take on a note of madness as it grows in scope.

"You shall not bear false witness against your neighbor" (Ex. 20:16).

"What is man that you are mindful of him,
and the son of man that thou dost care for him?
For thou hast made him little less than God,
and dost crown him with glory and honor (Ps. 8:4-5).
Why would one person with a harsh word destroy another
before one's peers when both are the creation of the same
beneficent hand of God?

The truth spoken about another makes a friend forever, but a
falsehood builds the path toward hatred.

The word of kindness spoken about the neighbor blesses both
the speaker and the hearer, for it lifts both in the dignity of
human life.

The love of fellow human beings is most evident in their kind
word spoken not to their faces but behind their backs.

"You shall not bear false witness against your neighbor" (Ex.
20:16).

"What man is there who desires life,
    and covets many days, that he may enjoy good?
Keep your tongue from evil,
    and your lips from speaking deceit" (Ps. 34:12-13).
Honesty in speaking about another builds quiet relaxation and joy into our lives. This is because truth bears its own reward of contentment.

Life is brief, and the wise person realizes there are no days so useless that they can be wasted in attacks on another's character.

"For thou hast made him a little lower than the angels" (Ps. 8:5, KJV).
If God is mindful of the possibilities of humans, why should humans be less aware? To recognize the honor and strength of another and to speak of these characteristics throughout the land is the mark of God upon the life.

"You shall not bear false witness against your neighbor" (Ex. 20:16).

"It is the Spirit himself bearing witness with our spirit that we are children of God, and if children, then heirs, heirs of God and fellow heirs with Christ, provided we suffer with him, in order that we may also be glorified with him" (Rom. 8:16-17). When we consider the relationship of joint heirship, it indeed seems foolish to attack another with whom we share so much of our being.

To be a child of God is sufficient; there is no need to attempt to rob another of his dignity in order to gain some imagined advantage in life.

The saddest act of thievery is the theft of reputation.

"You shall not bear false witness against your neighbor" (Ex. 20:16).

"When they had assembled with the elders and taken counsel, they gave a sum of money to the soldiers and said, "Tell people, 'His disciples came by night and stole him away while we were asleep.' And if this comes to the governor's ears, we will satisfy him and keep you out of trouble" (Matt. 28:12-14).

The results of swearing to false information touched heavily the lives of Jesus, Stephen, and Paul. Here it touched the soldiers at the empty tomb. Always the results are the same: darkness, sadness, and despair. On the other hand the carrying of a truthful witness brings joy and peace. The contrast is evident in every case.

To build, whether it is a structure or another's life, requires artistic skill. To destroy requires only brute action.

"You shall not bear false witness against your neighbor" (Ex. 20:16).

12

Positive Power from the
Tenth Commandment
Find Contentment and Joy in Your
Own Possessions

"You shall not covet" (Ex. 20:17).

Viewpoint

The Tenth Commandment falls into a unique category since it deals so specifically with a mental attitude rather than an overt action such as stealing or murder. Also, the prohibited act does not necessarily injure another; in fact, the owner of the coveted property may not even be aware of the envy directed toward him or her.

This command is literally a kind admonition against harming ourselves with the destructive force of envy and bitterness which accompany greed for something which is not our own. It is a command against inappropriate thoughts, and a positive view of its meaning presents it as a command to bless our own lives by thinking kindly and wisely where another's family and property are concerned.

Pressed into this command is the familiar thought of Acts 20:35*b* which states that it is more blessed to give than to receive. Perhaps even the opposite of *covet* might be thought of as "give," for the word *covet* speaks of taking or of wishing to take, and "give" is the outreaching in the opposite direction.

The list of holdings which we are commanded to avoid coveting ranges through house, marriage partners, servants, and animals which were often the measure of property in biblical life. The list sounds surprisingly modern to us, and maybe we would only need to add automobiles and clothing to make the picture complete in our minds.

It is easy to think of coveting quite lightly, almost as though the word itself could be defined as admiring or appreciating. But such a definition is not borne out by either the dictionary or by Bible references.

The dictionary uses harsh terms such as desiring inordinately and also of desiring without due regard to the rights of others. When we accept this definition we realize we are treading closely to the thought of outright theft or fraud in order to secure the property of another.

Paul's references tie covetousness closely to idolatry as he says in Colossians 3:5: "Put to death therefore what is earthly in you . . . and covetousness, which is idolatry." He again uses the same terminology in Ephesians 5:5. It is easy to see the connection between covetousness and idolatry since the adoration of any object to the point of excess can easily form that object into an idol, and this connection undoubtedly was the source of the original command from God.

Happily, God's desire for us is always the avenue of goodness, and His exhortation to turn from an evil is as surely an urging to turn toward a good. And in this case, that good which places our minds in a contented perspective might well be expanded by the words of Romans 8:32 which point us toward God's overpowering willingness freely to "give us all things with him." It is shortsighted at best to consider inordinately desiring another's property when God has expressed His own desire to give us individually all of the good things of earth and heaven. The availability of such gifts in our lives reduces to nothing the inclination to covet what another may have. God's provision makes a mockery of our covetousness.

Again, His infinite positive mind and message cry to us, "I have already provided all things for you. I am your Source, and the property of another person is meaningless to you. Your needs, as well as your joy, are my concern. Look to Me."

Removal of covetousness, like removal of weeds from a garden, is not accomplished in a moment's time, for the roots grow deep and strong.

But the two-pronged tools of appreciation and thankfulness for that which is our own, will work skillfully to cut away the roots of the plant of envy with its flower of covetousness.

Jesus commands us to love others as ourselves, and as difficult to achieve as this is, the rewards in happiness are apparent.

One of the rewards is the ability to enjoy good things coming to others. This attitude is an opposite of covetousness.

"Keep your life free from love of money, and be content with what you have; for he has said, 'I will never fail you nor forsake you' " (Heb. 13:5).

God's order of action here is first for controlling covetousness, then for seeking contentment. He sets priorities to help us think more lucidly.

"You shall not covet" (Ex. 20:17).

When we mentally and emotionally grant each other steward-ship of the gracious things of life, we begin to understand God's ownership of the earth and His constant acts of sharing His abundant gifts with us.

God's hand holds all riches, and the fingers open widely to let blessings fall into the lives of His people. This openhandedness is God's example of sharing. It is a pattern carefully designed for each of us to follow.

As powerful anticipation of the blessings of God comes into our individual lives, the inclination to begrudge another his posses-sions drifts into nothingness.

All commands of God point to contentment, and contentment which flourishes in the mind rules out craving for that which is not our own.

"You shall not covet" (Ex. 20:17).

Remedies are usually available, but they are seldom easy to utilize. The psalmist offered his remedy for covetousness in straightforward words as he wrote,

"Incline my heart to thy testimonies,
   and not to gain" (Ps. 119:36).

The secret of the remedy is in the words, "Incline my heart" for all else follows when the heart leads the way toward God.

Ownership of beautiful things adds brightness and comfort to life, but the heart that forgets all else fails to develop its possibility for peace.

Contentment and envy are mutually exclusive characteristics. We each must decide which trait we most want in our lives.

"You shall not covet" (Ex. 20:17).

Exodus 18:21 presents a seldom-recognized possibility as it states that men chosen for authority must not only be free of covetousness but actually hate its presence. Perhaps in God's eyes this is a requirement for leadership. The Scripture reads: "Moreover choose able men from all the people, such as fear God, men who are trustworthy and who hate a bribe; and place such men over the people as rulers of thousands, of hundreds, of fifties, and of tens."

To yearn to achieve all that is possible within us is a wholesome characteristic of mind, and to yearn for others to achieve all that is in them is the mark of God's mind at work within us.

"You shall not covet" (Ex. 20:17).

"But earnestly desire the higher gifts" (1 Cor. 12:31a).
In some translations "earnestly desire" appears as "covet."
This verse may illustrate one of the few valid areas for covetousness—that of those gifts from God which defraud no one.

The greatest tool for removing covetousness from the life is an ever-developing awareness and thankfulness for the things God has given to each of us.

God's gifts to us are so good, and we see His hand so clearly at work among us in the richness not only of our own lives but also in other lives, that justification for covetousness becomes impossible to discover in the Christian life.

"You shall not covet" (Ex. 20:17).

13

The First and Greatest Commandment of Jesus

"You shall love the Lord your God with all your heart . . .
and your neighbor as yourself" (Mark 12:30a,31a).

Viewpoint

The greatest commandment, the summary commandment, the powerful commandment, the positive commandment—this was given by Jesus. He combined all laws under a double heading: love God and love your fellowman. His powerful words distill the first four Commandments concerning loving and worshiping God into the first sentence as He said in Mark 12:29-30: "The first is, 'Hear, O Israel: The Lord our God, the Lord is one; and you shall love the Lord your God with all your heart, and with all your soul, and with all your mind, and with all your strength.' "

In equally concise fashion He combines the six human relationship commandments dealing with parents, murder, adultery, theft, bearing false witness, and coveting into the simple instruction, "The second is this, 'You shall love your neighbor as yourself." There is no other commandment greater than these" (Mark 12:31).

None but the mind of God could include so much comprehensive teaching about the way people are to live gloriously and abundantly in God's path on God's earth. And no other could have expressed so completely the teaching that all goodness hangs on a single, scarlet rope of love.

He is telling us that all actions have their beginning in the mind and heart, and human worship which comes from the heart is the holy concern of God. "Love," He says, and "Love again," for "God is love." These are only words until slowly they find their way into our lives with the realization that He places his love in the human mind to make good, constructive, wholesome action possible.

As is always true of God's dealing with us, He does not give commands and then leave us to work out our methods of obedience as best we can. He does not say, "Love!" and then withdraw; instead, He Himself creates the love within us through the power of the Holy Spirit. This is the love which motivates, the love which shapes a life to God's specifications.

It is interesting that Jesus spoke this command of love in unpleasant, unsympathetic circumstances. The Pharisees, Sadducees, Herodians, and scribes came to Him as He taught and attempted to find errors and self-condemning statements in His speech. They asked complicated questions about taxes to Caesar, about the status of marriage relationships after the resurrection, and then they asked the question about identifying the "first" commandment.

Each of the questions was argumentative and allowed for no simple, satisfactory answer, yet Jesus answered so wisely that "after that no one dared to ask him any question" (Mark 12:34).

Probably as the inquirers posed the questions, they were supposing they could worry Jesus into saying that it was more important to avoid murder or perhaps stealing. With any answer there would have been unlimited opportunity for debate

and accusation. But Jesus brushed it all aside with the reminder
that love was the answer which covered all actions.

How strange this talk of love must have sounded to critics
eager to create a battlefield rather than a platform for learning
about God.

Jesus speaks of all Commandments with honor since they are
valuable to all people in the shaping of life, and in John 13:34
He speaks of a "new commandment." "A new commandment
I give to you, that you love one another; even as I have loved
you, that you also love one another."

Certainly the thought of love is not "new"; it was a part of
the very first of the Ten Commandments. Where is the newness
then? Why did He tell us He was giving a "new" commandment?

Many things come to mind which are different and new, and
each adds an insight to His teaching of love. The command is
from a new Lawgiver, not Moses but Jesus, and in this respect
it is new. Also, the command has a new context as it commands
a mutual love. It does not speak of loving your neighbor but
rather of loving one another. Here the action is seen as a shared
act: you love, and your neighbor loves.

Further, the example of the Savior's love is introduced as He
says we are to love "as I have loved you." Here is a deep avowal
of the personal love of Jesus for us, and this adds a newness.
It is literally an outpouring of love from Jesus to us. It culmi-
nates in the command for us to love others because of His love
which is that greatest love expressed in giving His life for us.
These are all words to be recalled through the ages in answer
to the question of whether God does in fact actually love His
children. He does, and this love is the motive for our love for
others. There is divine logic here, for without His love as the
pattern and guide for life, our love for others would be at best
a weak production.

Love, then, is seen as the new commandment, and it is also

seen as the old commandment from the mind of God. Each of the Ten Commandments produces acts of helpfulness and care, but Jesus' words go to the heart of loving care because they are a part of the description of our loving God.

The truly good life, in the deepest sense of the term, lies deep in every command of the Bible. It is God speaking from the deep fullness of all wisdom, and His message is clear to us on a simple daily basis as He might speak to each of us, "Obey Me. I know the way of love. Let Me reveal it to each of you, for herein lies contentment and joy. This is My plan and purpose for your life. My instruction is given for your growth and understanding. Hear Me, for I am God."

"But the fruit of the Spirit is love, joy, peace, patience, kindness, goodness, faithfulness, gentleness, self-control; against such there is no law" (Gal. 5:22-23).

The source of the love in our lives must be the Holy Spirit, for God is the Source of all creation, and love is the highest expression of His work.

"Owe no one anything except to love one another; for he who loves his neighbor has fulfilled the law" (Rom. 13:8).

Here is all of life's motivation condensed into a single thought. Even as God's very mind itself is too large for our understanding, so here the thought can only be accepted with the trust that we will grow into a deeper realization of the meaning of the words we read and repeat with awe.

"And you shall love the Lord your God with all your heart . . . and your neighbor as yourself" (Mark 12:30a).

Love is a way of life. In fact, it is life. Its reward is peace, and it has no penalty.

Love looks both inward and outward. The inward view gives strength and direction. The outward view presents opportunity for expression and development; and not to be overlooked, it gives opportunity for service.

We walk in a tradition of love, one that began long before human beings were created.
"For the Father loves the Son, and shows him all that he himself is doing; and greater works than these will he show him, that you may marvel" (John 5:20).

"And you shall love the Lord your God with all your heart . . . and your neighbor as yourself" (Mark 12:30a).

To think of the Old Testament as harsh and warring is to miss the deep presence of love in the simple statements regarding homelife.

"Better is a dinner of herbs where love is, than a fatted ox and hatred with it" (Prov. 15:17).

The dictionary includes in its definition of love the thought of doing good for others, not merely of feeling good toward them. In so doing, it has explained love as a kind of action which springs from a deep desire to elevate the life of others in whatever areas their needs may exist.

"Truly, I say to you, as you did it to one of the least of these my brethren, you did it to me" (Matt. 25:40b).

"And you shall love the Lord your God with all your heart . . . and your neighbor as yourself (Mark 12:30a).

"I led them with cords of compassion,
   with bands of love" (Hos. 11:4).
God speaks of drawing Israel with "bands of love." Here is
gentleness and care reminiscent of Jesus' care of His disciples,
a care which held them, as it holds us, at His side for all times.

Where the voice of God is heard, there are expressions of love.
How could it be otherwise when He defines Himself as love?
"The Lord appeared to him from afar. I have loved you with
an everlasting love" (Jer. 31:3).

Love is the invention and production of God Himself. Without
Him, each would understand only those things which contrib-
ute to his own comfort and well-being.

"And you shall love the Lord your God with all your heart
. . . and your neighbor as yourself" (Mark 12:30a).

"Greater love has no man than this, that a man lay down his life for his friends" (John 15:13).

I learned this Scripture in a fifth-grade reading class when we read together the story of a man who gave his life to save another. I did not know until much later that this word was from the Bible, and even more that it was a reminder of Christ's giving His life for us. It applies on all levels because it is totally true.

"By this all men will know that you are my disciples, if you have love for one another" (John 13:35).

It is a living definition of Christians that they have love for others.

We often learn slowly the valuable lessons of God, but even the partial lessons of love which we master make all the difference between contentment and despair.

"And you shall love the Lord your God with all your heart . . and your neighbor as yourself" (Mark 12:30a).

"Love does no wrong to a neighbor; therefore love is the fulfilling of the law" (Rom. 13:10).

Here is the single sentence which explains the Ten Commandments. To do no harm to others and always to do well for them: this fulfills the intent of the law.

Remove the word *love* from the Bible, and there remains only a lengthy story of people grasping and fighting their way through endless days.

Love makes all the difference, and love is the reason for the actions of God and of those whose lives He touches and indwells.

"And you shall love the Lord your God with all your heart . . . and your neighbor as yourself" (Mark 12:30*a*).

"Love is patient and kind; love is not jealous or boastful; it is not arrogant or rude. Love does not insist on its own way; it is not irritable or resentful; it does not rejoice at wrong, but rejoices in the right. Love bears all things, believes all things, hopes all things, endures all things" (1 Cor. 13:4-7).

In this great chapter of 1 Corinthians are listed the characteristics of love. Nowhere else have they ever been recorded so completely. This is not surprising when we remember that love is the core of all biblical understanding.

The many kinds of love are discussed in songs and stories, and none should be scorned. But to move from the level of pure emotion to the level of placing the needs of another first is a step toward God's maturity.

"And you shall love the Lord your God with all your heart . . . and your neighbor as yourself" (Mark 12:30*a*).

14

A Galaxy of Scriptures
Regarding the Law

"Teacher, which is the great commandment in the law?" And he said to him, "You shall love the Lord your God with all your heart, and with all your soul, and with all your mind. This is the great and first commandment. And a second is like it, You shall love your neighbor as yourself. On these two commandments depend all the law and the prophets" (Matt. 22:36-40).

If you really fulfil the royal law, according to the scripture, "You shall love your neighbor as yourself," you do well (Jas. 2:8).

The law of his God is in his heart;
    his steps do not slip (Ps. 37:31).

I delight to do thy will, O my God:
    thy law is within my heart (Ps. 40:8).

Let thy mercy come to me, that I may live;
    for thy law is my delight (Ps. 119:77).

Hearken to me, you who know righteousness,
    the people in whose heart is my law;
fear not the reproach of men,
    and be not dismayed at their revilings.
For the moth will eat them up like a garment,
    and the worm will eat them like wool;

But my deliverance will be for ever,
and my salvation to all generations (Isa. 51:7-8).

Unless thy law had been my delight,
I should have perished in my affliction
(Ps. 119:92).

Oh, how I love thy law!
It is my mediation all the day (Ps. 119:97).

I hate double-minded men,
but I love thy law (Ps. 119:113).

For the law of the Spirit of life in Christ Jesus has made me free from the law of sin and death (Rom. 8:2).

For I delight in the law of God in my inmost self, but I see in my members another law, at war with the law of my mind and making me captive to the law of sin which is in my members (Rom. 7:22-23).

Great peace have those who love thy law;
nothing can make them to stumble (Ps. 119:165).

I long for thy salvation, O Lord,
and thy law is my delight (Ps. 119:174).

True instruction was in his mouth, and no wrong was found on his lips. He walked with me in peace and uprightness, and he turned many from iniquity (Mal. 2:6).

But he who looks into the perfect law, the law of liberty, and perseveres, being no hearer that forgets but a doer that acts, he shall be blessed in his doing (Jas. 1:25).

So speak and so act as those who are to be judged under the law of liberty (Jas. 2:12).

If you really fulfil the royal law according to the scripture, "You shall love your neighbor as yourself," you do well (Jas. 2:8).

"All things are lawful for me," but not all things are helpful. "All things are lawful for me," but I will not be enslaved by anything (1 Cor. 6:12).

Blessed is the man
    who walks not in the counsel of the wicked,
    nor stands in the way of sinners,
    nor sits in the seat of scoffers,
but his delight is in the law of the Lord;
    and on his law he meditates day and night.
He is like a tree
    planted by the streams of water,
that yields its fruit in its season,
    and its leaf does not wither.
In all that he does, he prospers (Ps. 1:1-4).

Understanding this, that the law is not laid down for the just but for the lawless and disobedient, for the ungodly and sinners, for the unholy and profane, for murderers of fathers and murderers of mothers, for manslayers (1 Tim. 1:9).

For no human being will be justified in his sight by works of the law, since through the law comes knowledge of sin (Rom. 3:20).

For the law was given through Moses; grace and truth came through Jesus Christ (John 1:17).

Let it be known to you therefore, brethren, that through this man forgiveness of sins is proclaimed to you, and by him every one that believes is freed from everything from which you could not be freed by the law of Moses (Acts 13:38-39).

(For the law made nothing perfect); on the other hand, a better hope is introduced, through which we draw near to God (Heb. 7:19).

Think not that I have come to abolish the law and the prophets; I have come not to abolish them but to fulfil them (Matt. 5:17).

Woe to you, scribes and Pharisees, hypocrites! for you tithe mint and dill and cummin, and have neglected the weightier matters of the law, justice and mercy and faith; these you ought to have done, without neglecting the others (Matt. 23:23).

The law of the Lord is perfect,
    reviving the soul;
the testimony of the Lord is sure,
    making wise the simple;
The precepts of the Lord are right,

rejoicing the heart;
the commandment of the Lord is pure,
    enlightening the eyes (Ps. 19:7-8).

We know that the law is good, if any one uses it lawfully (1 Tim. 1:8).

The law was our custodian until Christ came, that we might be justified by
faith (Gal. 3:24).

For all the law if fulfilled in one word, "You shall love your neighbor as
yourself" (Gal. 5:14).

Bear one another's burdens, and so fulfil the law of Christ (Gal. 6:2).

Law came in, to increase the trespass; but where sin increased, grace abound-
ed all the more (Rom. 5:20).

When they had appointed a day for him, they came to him at his lodging in
great number. And he expounded the matter to them from morning till
evening, testifying to the kingdom of God and trying to convince them about
Jesus both from the law of Moses and from the prophets (Acts 28:23).

For he is our peace, who has made us both one, and has broken down the
dividing wall of hostility, by abolishing in his flesh the law of commandments
and ordinances, that he might create in himself one new man in place of the
two, so making peace (Eph. 2:14-15).

For Christ is the end of the law that every one who has faith may be justified
(Rom. 10:4).

Christ redeemed us from the curse of the law, having become a curse for
us—for it is written, "Cursed be every one who hangs on a tree" (Gal. 3:13).

[Knowing] that a man is not justified by the works of the law, but through
faith in Jesus Christ, even we have believed in Christ Jesus, in order to be
justified by faith in Christ, and not by works of the law, because by works
of the law shall no one be justified (Gal. 2:16).

No man is justified before God by the law; for "He who through faith is
righteous shall live" (Gal. 3:11).

What then shall we say? That the law is sin? By no means! Yet, if it had not
been for the law, I should not have known sin. I should not have known what
it is to covet if the law had not said, "You shall not covet" (Rom. 7:7).

So the law is holy, and the commandment holy and just and good (Rom. 7:12).

We know that the law is spiritual; but I am carnal, sold under sin. For what I am doing, I do not understand my own actions. For I do not do what I want, but I do the very thing I hate. Now if I do what I do not want, I agree that the law is good (Rom. 7:14-16).

Ezra opened the book in the sight of all the people, for he was above all the people, and when he opened it all the people stood (Neh. 8:5). And they read from the book, from the law of God, clearly, and they gave the sense, so that the people understood the reading (v. 8).

For Christ is the end of the law, that every one who has faith may be justified (Rom. 10:4).

The law does not rest on faith, for "He who does them shall live by them" (Gal. 3:12).

But when the time had fully come, God sent forth his Son, born of woman, born under the law, to redeem those who were under the law, so that we might receive adoption as sons (Gal. 4:4-5).

But if you are led by the Spirit you are not under the law (Gal. 5:18).